K is for Kissing a Cool Kangaroo

For Mary – G.A.

For Pam and John Hodgson, salt of the earth – G.P.-R.

ORCHARD BOOKS
338 Euston Road, London NW1 3BH
Hachette Children's Books
Orchard Books Australia
Level 17/207 Kent Street, Sydney, NSW 2000
First published in Great Britain in 2002
First paperback publication in 2003
ISBN 1 84121 262 8
13 digit ISBN 9781841212623
Text © Purple Enterprises 2002
Illustrations © Guy Parker-Rees 2002
The rights of Giles Andreae to be identified as the author and
Guy Parker-Rees to be identified as the illustrator of this Work
have been asserted by them in accordance with the
Copyright, Designs and Patents Act, 1988.
A CIP catalogue record for this book is available from the British Library
7 9 10 8
Printed in China

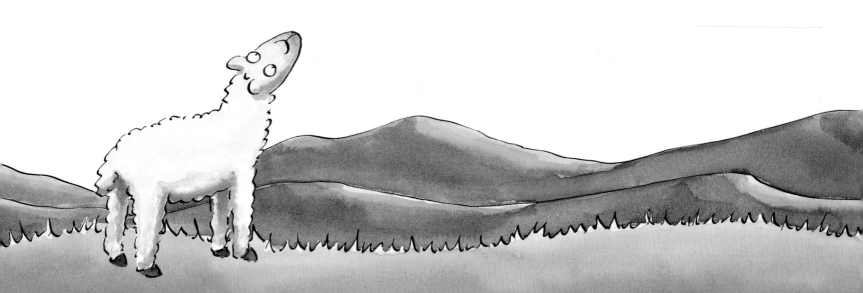

K is for Kissing a Cool Kangaroo

Giles Andreae — Guy Parker-Rees

ORCHARD BOOKS

b is for **busy** and **big bumble-bee**

Bb

C c

c is for **cat** who has got all the **cream**

d is for **dragonfly**, **daisy** and **dream**

e is for **elephant**, mighty and strong

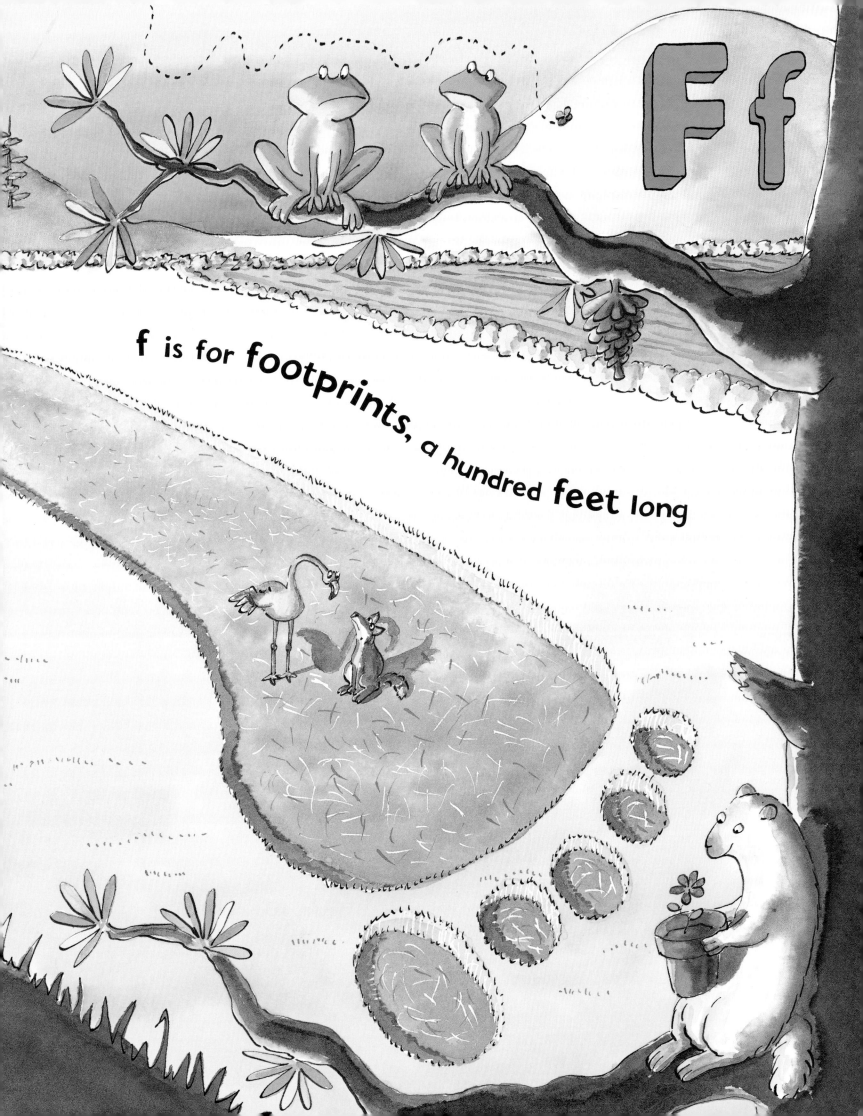

f is for **footprints**, a hundred **feet** long

Gg

g is for **giant**, whose **garden grows** wild

Hh

h is for **holding** the **hand** of a child

Ii

i is for **igloo**, a house made of **ice**

j is for **jellybeans** – ooh, they're so nice!

K k

k is for **kissing** a cool **kangaroo**

l is for **loving**, like Daddy **loves** you

M m

m is for **mischievous monkey** and **mat**

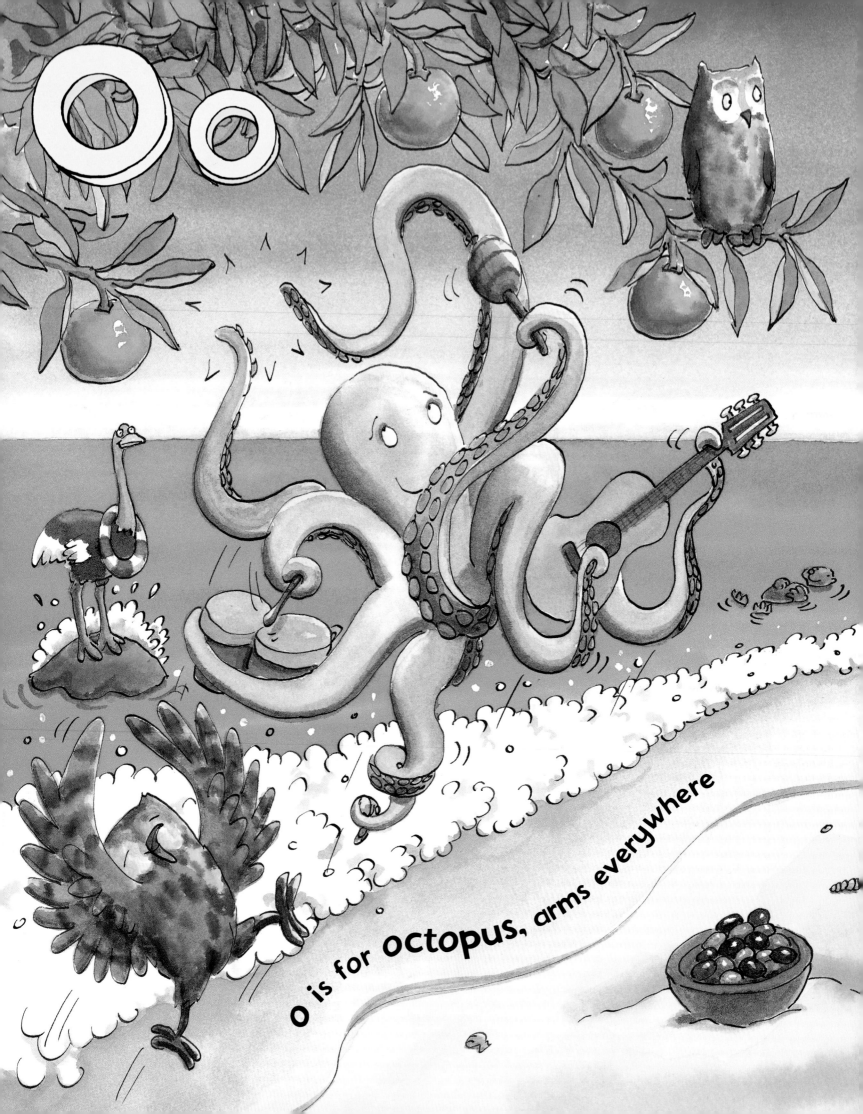

O is for **octopus**, arms everywhere

P is for **peaceful** and **piglet** and **pear**

q is for "Quickly, I've cuddled the **Queen!**"

r is for **robot** and **racing** machine

S is for **snowman** and **sister** and **snake**

t is for **teatime**, so let's have some cake!

u is for **uncle** and **udder** and **up**

V is for **vampire** with blood in his cup

w whispers and waves you goodbye

Yy

y is for **yeti** and **yoyo** and **yes**

Zz

and Z is for zebra – now how did you guess?!

There are lots of other things on every page you may have missed.

See if you can find them . . . then check them on this list!

Aa
armadillo

antelope

ant

beetle

bull

Bb
balloon

Cc
cake

caterpillar

clouds

dalmatian

dog

Dd
duck

Ee
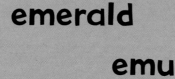

emerald

emu

eagle

frog

ferret

Ff
flamingo

Gg

goat

gnu

giraffe

house

hamster

hyena

Hh

Ii

icicle

iguana

ibis

jester

jaguar

jam

Jj

llama

koala

Ll

Kk

kitten

kiwi

ladybird

lynx

Mm

milk

mango

mole

nectarine

newt

nest

Nn

Oo

owl

olives

otter

pelican

porcupine

pirate ship

Pp

Qq

quiche

quail

quiver

raccoon

rose

Rr

rat

Ss

skunk

seal

salamander

toucan

Tt

teddy

turtle

Uu

unicorn

umbrella

vulture

violet

Vv

vole

Ww

weasel

woodpecker

wombat

x-ray

Xx

Yy

yak

yellowhammer

zinnia

Zz